Almost Like Home

A Family Guide to Navigating the Nursing Home Maze

Joanna R. Leefer

MJN PUBLISHING

Almost Like Home: A Family Guide to Navigating the Nursing Home Maze.

CONTENTS

PREFACE

Seldom will you hear a person say that he or she wants to live in a senior residence or nursing home. Likewise, many people cannot imagine ever allowing their loved one to be placed into a home. But when faced with the responsibilities of providing 24-hour care for an aging person with ever-increasing physical needs beyond what one person can physically handle, a nursing home frequently becomes the best alternative.

Nursing homes can conjure up scary images. Part of the fear is based on the notion that these are places people go to die. But this does not necessarily need to be the case! Many people continue to live, and in fact, live better in a nursing facility than they would at home. Constant care, meals, housekeeping, activities, and even the opportunity to connect with other residents and develop new friends and interests are all provided.

It takes work to navigate the nursing home maze and find the best facility and make it into a home for your loved one. I designed this book to help families go through this process. I am fortunate to have gained a thorough overview of how to do this, through my own personal experience, and my training as a professional senior care advisor.

In this book, you will find step-by-step guidelines for helping you select the right facility where your loved one's needs will be met, along with tips for getting him or her into the home of your choice. I will provide behind-the-scenes information on how a nursing home runs, along with checklists on what to look for, questions to ask, and factors that need to be considered when selecting a facility. Also included are advocacy tips (using official and unofficial channels) to ensure that your loved one receives optimal care. And I provide steps to take if you feel their care is inadequate.

The book is user-friendly and has been designed so you can easily go to the section you need and readily find the information you are seeking without wading through endless text. The language is simple and easy to comprehend.

In many instances, families are unable to anticipate their loved one's eldercare needs until they are face-to-face with a crisis. If you are in a caregiver role, the best advice I can give to you is to start looking at your options before the situation becomes critical. By doing your homework upfront and understanding your options, you will be able to make an educated decision, rather than working on impulse if suddenly faced with a crisis.

I offer you this guide in hopes that it will help you through what can be a daunting process. What better way to show your love for someone than by investigating the best care options for their older years? And take it from me, when you do find the right place, it will bring you great peace of mind.

A NOTE TO READERS

Nursing homes are regulated on both the federal and state level. All states must adhere to basic federal regulations. Although the fundamental structures are the same, states can differ somewhat in supervision. This book offers information that is relevant to all states. Most of my examples specifically address New York nursing homes, because that is the state in which I have the most experience. However, I have included a guide to resources or websites that will provide detailed information for all states.

INTRODUCTION

My sister, brother, and I swore we would do everything we could before we placed our parents in any type of care facility. As my mother's Alzheimer's disease progressed, she lost all sense of time and wandered around the house day and night. We removed the dials from the stove so she would not try to cook and we put locks high on the outside doors so she would not go outside. Even with all these precautions, her erratic behavior began to wear my father down, and his health began to suffer.

Reluctantly, we decided to look for a facility where my mother would be safe and my father would have some companionship. After two unsuccessful attempts, and much trial and error, we settled on a facility that had a small studio apartment for my father and a dementia floor for my mother. They could spend time together during the day, but would be separated at night. This seemed like the ideal solution. Our mother could walk around at any time during the day or night and be under the watchful eye of the 24-hour staff. My father could get a full night of sleep.

Separating my parents at night was one of our biggest fears. My parents were very close and they were rarely apart. The first few days at the facility were frightening for everyone. There were many questions: Would my mother get confused when my father left in the evening? How would my father react to the separation?

We were cautious at first. The entire family planned to visit daily and stay until bedtime. We wanted to be sure that our parents were comfortable in their new surroundings. However, the staff was professional and firm, providing strong directives. The first night, my dad said goodnight and went to his own apartment. The next day, we found our mother not upset at all. When she saw my father come out of the elevator, she announced to anyone within listening distance: "Here comes Bernie. He is my sweetheart." She walked up to him as though they were never separated. We had faced our fear of the worst scenario and it turned out okay.

CHAPTER 1

WHAT IS A NURSING HOME?

First things first. Before you begin, you must determine if a nursing home best suits your needs. A nursing home, also known as a Skilled Nursing Facility (SNF), is a residential facility that provides room and board, around-the-clock nursing care, rehabilitation services, personal-care services, medically related social services, and recreational and social activities. While all nursing homes must provide certain basic services, some may provide specialized care for specific types of medical conditions, such as services for people with head injuries, ventilator dependence, bariatric needs, AIDS, or mental health issues. It is important to know exactly what type of care your loved one requires before starting a nursing home search.

Nursing home care can be very expensive if paid for privately. The average cost ranges from $10,000–$15,000 per month. However, most patients entering a skilled facility have their expenses covered by

Joanna R. Leefer

Institutional Medicaid, which is a federal program administered at the state level that provides health care for low-income individuals.

That does not mean you have to be destitute to get Institutional Medicaid. A person entering a nursing home can "spend down." Middle- and upper-income individuals, for example, can become eligible for Institutional Medicaid by transferring savings and assets to a third party five years before entering a nursing home and can still be eligible for Medicaid. (I will explain Institutional Medicaid later in the book.)

PROS AND CONS OF NURSING HOME CARE

Unfortunately, nursing homes in general have a bad reputation, in part due to unfavorable media coverage and negative word-of-mouth stories. But remember, most people are more interested in a story about someone suing a facility because a loved one fell and broke a hip than a tale about employees who volunteer their time to ensure a dying resident is not alone. Stories like that never make the headlines! You need to know that there are many, many more good facilities than bad ones.

Before embarking on a search for the best facility for your loved one, it is important to know the pros and cons of nursing home care and whether they mesh with your family's needs. Following are some important considerations.

MAJOR ADVANTAGES:

- Government oversight: Any nursing home that receives Medicare and Medicaid funds must pass stringent inspection standards every 12 to 15 months. This means there are standards of care that the facility must abide by.

- 24-hour skilled nursing care: This is helpful for individuals who need medical supervision both day and night.

- Attention to daily needs: Housekeeping, meals and grooming are provided

- Less intervention by you, the caregiver: Daily care is the responsibility of the nursing home staff, allowing you to spend more quality time with your loved one and to attend to your other personal responsibilities.

- A social network: Meals, activities, doctor visits are all available at the facility.

MAJOR DISADVANTAGES:

- Lack of privacy: Many facilities do not offer private rooms, so residents may have to share a room with at least one other person.

- Lack of autonomy: Other people will make decisions on aspects of your loved one's daily routine (although family input is often considered)

Joanna R. Leefer

Institutional setting: Residents can bring a few personal possessions, but space will be limited, so they may not be allowed to bring many items.

Nursing Home Care	
PROS	**CONS**
Government Regulated: Accepts Medicare and Medicaid	Institutional Setting
24-Hour Skilled Nursing Care	No One-on-One Attention
Offers a Social Network	Lack of Privacy and Shared Spaces
Includes Housekeeping, Assistance with Meals, and Grooming	Lack of Autonomy/ Independence
Reduced Family Responsibility in Providing Care	More Isolation from Family

CHAPTER 2

CHOOSING THE RIGHT NURSING HOME

STARTING THE SEARCH:
UPFRONT CONSIDERATIONS

Starting to search for the right nursing home for a loved one can seem daunting Before starting the process, take some time to consider the following:

#1 FINANCIAL CONSIDERATIONS

As mentioned in Chapter 1, a skilled nursing facility can be very expensive if paid for privately. Six months of nursing home care can cost over $50,000. Not many people can afford these payments over a long period of time. However, most patients entering a skilled care facility have their expenses covered by Institutional Medicaid.

In order to qualify for Medicaid a person must fit the following criteria:

- Be 65 or older or disabled as determined by Social Security criteria.
- Be a U.S. citizen or qualified non-citizen.
- Fall below a predetermined federal/state income and asset level.

(To learn more about Medicaid eligibility, go to Appendix B.)

Many people mistakenly think Medicare covers nursing home stays. In fact, Medicare covers only temporary skilled care, usually in the rehabilitation section of a nursing home.

HOW TO QUALIFY FOR
INSTITUTIONAL MEDICAID

Every state has its own income/asset eligibility criteria for Medicaid, but you do not necessarily need to be destitute to qualify. You can become eligible for maintenance services if you transfer your assets to someone else **five years before you need nursing home care.** This five- year requirement is called the "look back" period. A person who enters a home before the look back period is reached must pay a significant monetary penalty before she can begin receiving Medicaid benefits.

It is best to consult an elder law attorney in your state to determine your loved one's eligibility requirements and whether there are some incomes and assets that might be exempt.

 *Author's Note*
To find out your state's Medicaid requirement, contact your state's Medicaid department or search the Internet under your state and "Institutional Medicaid," e.g., "Institutional Medicaid + North Carolina."

I cannot emphasis enough the need to begin the "spend down" process early, at least five years before nursing home care is required. Many older people find it difficult to turn over their savings and assets to another person, even a family member, but the conversation is necessary. I have seen too many families shocked when they

25

Joanna R. Leefer

realize the money put aside for a grandchild's education had to be turned over to the government for nursing-home care.

#2: GEOGRAPHICAL CONSIDERATIONS

After finances, location should be your next consideration. You will want your loved one to be in a nursing home that is in a safe area, convenient to those who are most likely to visit.

3: MEDICAL CONSIDERATIONS

Many homes allow physicians privileges for patient visits. For continuity of care, it may be best to choose a home that your loved one's physician is affiliated with.

In addition, if your family member requires special equipment, such as a ventilator, you will need to find a nursing home that provides this service. If dementia care is needed, be sure to seek out facilities with well-regarded dementia programs. (For more information on Dementia Care, see CHAPTER 5.)

Hospice care is another factor worth considering. Not all facilities offer special end-of-life care. Another consideration often overlooked is weight. Obesity can present a challenge to some nursing homes while others offer special bariatric lifting equipment, wider beds, and stronger furniture to meet the needs of the very overweight.

#4: EMOTIONAL AND PRACTICAL CONSIDERATIONS

Next, you will want to consider your loved one's social and emotional needs to ensure he/she will feel comfortable in a new home.

Nursing home size and demographics are important. Will your loved one be happier in a small, intimate environment or in a larger facility that has state-of-the-art equipment and on-call medical specialists? If English is not your family member's first language, you may want to look into facilities where many staff members and residents speak his or her native language.

Consider, too, your family member's comfort level with living in a home that is affiliated with, or regulated by, a particular religious group. You should be aware that some religious facilities may have specific policies regarding end-of-life issues. Specifically, some may be unwilling to adhere to Do Not Resuscitate (DNR) orders or may not offer hospice care. Make sure these policies don't conflict with the wishes of your loved one.

#5: YOUR PERSONAL CONSIDERATIONS

Yes, you are a critical part of the choice equation and you, too, need to feel comfortable with the selected facility. Consider your own views on a home's administration, staff and policies, to ensure a good fit.

DEVELOPING A SHORT LIST

With key considerations in mind, it is time to use the following guidelines to develop a list of homes for consideration.

DETERMINE YOUR SEARCH AREA

It is important to determine who will most likely be visiting your loved one once he or she is placed in a home. Take a map and draw a circle, making the primary visitor's home the center. Determine the distance that person would be comfortable traveling on a regular basis to arrive at a search area. Be sure to consider how long it will take to get to a given home via car and/or public transportation.

CREATE A CHECKLIST

After you define your search area, make a list of all the nursing homes inside that zone. Sharpen your pencil and make a "spreadsheet" with a list of key considerations on the left side of the page and the names of all the area nursing homes on the top. The simple checklist on page 30 is a great place to start assessing how various homes meet your needs. Feel free to add other things that are important to you, to the bottom of the list.

To find nursing homes in your area, search online by specific township or zip code. One great resource is your state's Department of Health website; just search for nursing homes. In New York State, log on **to www.health.ny.gov/ facilities/nursing** to locate nursing homes by regions. For other states, input the state you live in as the search term along with "nursing home facility." You can also check the phone book, ask friends and neighbors for

Joanna R. Leefer

recommendations, or call a local hospital, adult daycare center, or senior community center and ask the medical staff or a social worker.

Once you compile a list of area nursing homes and key personal considerations, and preferences, you are ready to start your research. With all of the chart information filled in, you will be well on your way to narrowing down the list to a manageable number of homes.

Nursing Home Checklist			
	Nursing Home A	Nursing Home B	Nursing Home C
Miles from Home			
Private or Semi-Private Room			
Dementia Care			
Locked Unit for Safety			
Homey or Institutional Setting			
Physician Service			
Medical Needs			
Primary Language Spoken			
Religious Services			

VOICE OF EXPERIENCE
Appearance Is Not the Only Consideration

I remember the first time I had to select a nursing home for a client, whom I will refer to as Mrs. Taylor. Mrs. Taylor was in the early stages of Alzheimer's and needed a facility with an active Alzheimer's program and a good deal of space. She was a healthy person, and like many early Alzheimer's victims, she often became agitated and walked during all hours of the day and night.

One facility I visited was located by the ocean. It was a beautiful place. There was a view of the water and a balcony where family and residents could sit and sun themselves. The building was modern, clean, and outfitted with the latest in medical equipment. However, I slowly became aware that most of the staff, family, and residents spoke Russian. I could not ask questions of any of the families because English was not their first language.

Then it dawned on me that although the facility had many positives, my client would be out of place there. She and her family did not have a Russian background, did not know the language, and was unfamiliar with the culture. Even though the facility was suitable, the customs were not, so I crossed this facility off my selection list.

INVESTIGATING YOUR OPTIONS

With short list in hand, you can now begin an in-depth investigation of the facilities you are considering. The following six key resources can help you hone down your selection.

#1: PROMOTIONAL MATERIALS

Every nursing home has a brochure that lists services available at the facility. These are typically easy to obtain when you enter the building or by calling the marketing or admissions department and asking to have one mailed to you. The nursing home's website will also provide you with valuable information. Keep in mind that these materials are meant to "sell" the facility to the potential customer. So it's important not to make your decision based on this information alone. A nursing home will never advertise anything negative about its facility.

However, there are some basic facts you can glean from promotional materials. Brochures usually emphasize the facility's best- selling features. A home may have units that focus on a particular population, such as an Alzheimer's program or state-of-the art rehabilitation equipment. You may also learn if the facility promotes ethnic diversity or offers special services such as respite or hospice care.

Look at the photographs, but be aware that they are often generic pictures that the marketing department purchased, showing everybody happy and smiling, and may not be of actual people working or living in the facility. Let's be realistic, if all nursing homes looked as good as their brochures, we would never have a selection problem. We know that the reality is that all of those large spacious rooms may be photographed with wide-angle lenses, and the images of the expansive, outdoor areas neglect to show the highway running immediately behind the facility or the trash cans that were cropped out of the photo. You will get a truer picture if you visit the facility in person, or at least drive by.

#2: YOUR NETWORK

Word-of-mouth is one of your best sources of information. Talk to friends and family who have had an experience with a particular nursing home and get their opinion. You might consider talking to the staff at local senior centers or at social service agencies to get their thoughts. Hospital discharge planners may also have information on which facilities their patients prefer. If you belong to a club or church group, many times you will find people there who have had experience with nursing homes as well.

#3: INTERNET SOURCES

There are multiple websites that can provide information about nursing homes, such as the number of beds, types of equipment, services available, staff-to-patient ratio, etc. Some will offer summaries of the government's latest nursing home surveys. (see #4 below). (If you are technologically challenged, enlist help from your children, grandchildren, or the local library.)

Many of these sites include a comment section where readers can report their opinions and personal experiences regarding a facility. It's important to hear what they have to say.

Next, search local news sites for reports on nursing home events or conditions. News articles might report an innovative program the nursing home is introducing or cite any abuse identified within the facility. Any news is important.

#4: THE NURSING HOME SURVEY

Every nursing home that accepts Medicare or Medicaid must undergo a state inspection at least once every 12 to 15 months. The state typically sends a team of three to five employees who have a background in nursing, social work, dietetics, sanitation, health care administration, and counseling to conduct these surveys. The team walks through the facility, observes and evaluates on a checklist of approximately 150 regulatory standards. Some of these standards include physical and mental abuse, food preparation, and infection control, as well as clinical care standards.

When an inspection team finds that a home does not meet a specific regulation, it issues a citation indicating the number of times and severity of each deficiency. It then requests that the nursing home come up with a plan to remedy the situation. The written plan for correcting the deficiencies must be submitted within a predetermined time period.

If the nursing home does not correct its problem(s), The Center for Medicare and Medicaid Services (CMS) may end its agreement with the nursing home, which means the nursing home may lose Medicare and Medicaid funding and some of its residents will be transferred to other facilities.

Survey results are available online, although they are often difficult to locate. The best way to find a specific survey is to log on to your state's Department of Health website and enter a the name of the nursing home you are interested in, and the words, "Nursing Home Survey." You can also call the Department of Health and ask for a copy to be sent to you.

Tips On Reading A Nursing Home Survey

The nursing home survey may seem very confusing, but it can offer important insight into a nursing home's operation. Why? Because these surveys not only give ratings, they also offer specific reasons for the ratings; that is, they discuss the incidents that occurred and how the surveyor interpreted the data. In most cases you will agree with the surveyor's assessment—e.g., if several residents develop bedsores, everyone will agree that there is something basically amiss at the facility—but sometimes the incident is open to interpretation.

Any time an inspection team cites a deficiency, they give it a letter rating that indicates the frequency and severity of the deficiency. These letters span half of the alphabet. A "Level A" deficiency indicates an isolated incident with no actual harm. An example of a "Level A" deficiency is neglecting to place a required bulletin in the front lobby where everyone can see it.

The opposite extreme is a "Level I" deficiency. It indicates that there is a widespread possibility that a particular flaw might harm a significant number of residents. An example of a "Level I" would be the discovery of a dementia resident roaming the streets unattended, possibly indicating an extreme breach of the security system that could endanger many patients.

Most deficiencies are not so extreme, and some are open to interpretation. Levels A, B, and C are generally not considered significant; Levels D, E, and F are mid-range infringements; while Levels G, H, and I are very serious.

Author's Note

Some incidents that may not seem particularly harmful to one resident could be of significant concern to another. That is a good reason it is worth understanding the rating levels and how to interpret the comments. (For more detailed information on a nursing home survey, see Appendix C).

Cautions On Nursing Home Surveys

A nursing home survey is a snapshot, not a movie! While you may obtain considerable insight into health-safety factors, yet you must remember that it is only one of several reports to consider. A nursing home survey only offers a narrow window glimpse into how a nursing home operates; it cannot show what happens over a period of time.

Keep in mind that unannounced visits are not always unexpected! Theoretically, inspections come unannounced. However, nursing home personnel can often anticipate when an inspection will occur since it must be done every 12 to 15 months.

Also know that survey results are subject to interpretation! The interpretation of deficiency citations can vary. Similar deficiencies might be rated differently by individual surveyors depending upon how each situation is handled. Consider this situation: a resident with a swallowing problem is found choking, and the aide who has been assigned to help her is not around. Another sees her distress and helps. The situation was remedied and the patient has not sustained permanent harm. Is this a case of no actual harm or immediate jeopardy?

And recognize that a citation is only as good as the follow up handling of the infraction! The nursing home is required to come up with a written program of correction for a deficiency. Sometimes the survey team will revisit the facility to make sure that the plan has been initiated or that it has ultimately corrected the problem, but for less serious citations a "desk review" may be done. This means that someone at the state level reviews the paperwork and approves the facility's plan without returning to the facility to verify that it was implemented.

#5: THE "NURSING HOME COMPARE" DATABASE

An easier resource to use when evaluating nursing homes is a website that summarizes and compares nursing home survey results. This information is available to the public and is viewable online by going to **www.Medicare.gov/NursingHomeCompare**. You can select up to three nursing homes at a time and compare their ratings. Facilities are rated on a five-star measurement scale, with one star being the lowest rating and five stars the highest.

I advise you to consider only nursing homes with ratings of three stars or above, although there could be exceptions. If you are interested in a facility with a one- or two-star rating (maybe it is close to your home, or offers services you need, or a friend or family member works there), you should do a further investigation. This rating system is not fail-safe; it is only meant to be a guide.

Check out the comments the evaluators made and try to determine if their feedback pertains to issues that concern you or not. The book listing nursing home regulations is massive and lists requirements for everything from building maintenance, employee files, medical recordkeeping, as well as patient care.

Voice of Experience
Some Incidents Are More Personal Than Others

This particular incident occurred while I was working for FRIA, an advocacy organization for the elderly in New York City. I often scanned nursing home surveys to keep current on local nursing homes. I was reading a report about a particular nursing home that had a "Level B" rating in one area, indicating a slight infringement of the rules, but with no actual harm to a resident. Out of curiosity, I looked up the incident.

The incident involved a mix-up. Two male residents had died on the same day, and their bodies were placed in the nursing home's morgue. The funerals of both men were held on the same day, so two transports were sent out to deliver the bodies to their respective funeral homes. When the bodies were uncovered, the families discovered that each corpse had been mislabeled and delivered to the wrong family.

True, there was no actual harm to a resident since both men were deceased, but the impact on the families must have been overwhelming. This also left me with another concern: what kind of facility could be so impersonal that they were unable to identify a resident that had been part of the facility for several months? Yes, no actual harm had been done to a resident, but I felt that the incident revealed a more pressing concern. A misidentified resident, either dead or alive, indicates a staff that is not connected with its residents. To me this would be an excellent reason for not selecting this home.

After you have collected all the information, you can sit down with your checklist and eliminate the facilities that do not meet your needs or approval. Then compare the remaining facilities against the needs of your loved one and what is important to you. Make a list of any questions you may still have. Now that you've done your preliminary homework and identified nursing homes that meet your qualifications, it is time for some footwork.

#6: NURSING HOME TOURS

Touring the facility is a critical step in nursing home selection. A tour will give you a feeling for the facility and how it operates. It is a good idea to call the facility before you go. Many homes will give tours on the spot, but others schedule tours only on particular days and times.

Bring a companion, if possible. Two sets of eyes are better than one. After the tour, swap impressions. Take notes and ask plenty of questions.

A checklist can be helpful in evaluating a nursing home. On the next page, you will find some factors to consider for each place you visit. Look at the factors that should be considered when evaluating a nursing home. Some factors to consider are:

- Physical appearance of the facility both inside the building and outside

- The appearance of the residents -- Are they well cared for, or do they look neglected?

- Meal preparation and presentation

- Types of activities

- Interaction between staff and residents

For a more detailed checklist, see Appendix D. If you tour more than one nursing home, you might want to rate each factor on a scale of one to five, with one being the poorest and five being the best. This way you will have a measure of comparison.

SOME TOURING TIPS

When touring a home, always visit multiple floors or units and be sure to see more than the unit for "rehab" patients. The section used for rehabilitation is often more nicely furnished than the units for long-term residents because government reimbursements are higher for "rehab" patients, making these floors more profitable. Ask to see the unit where your loved one may be residing.

Note the interaction between staff and residents. "The resident always comes first!" should be the prevailing philosophy among all staff members. If your guide or another staff member ignores a distressed resident, this is cause for concern.

During your tour, note which rooms you are being shown. If you are brought into an occupied room unannounced or without permission, recognize that the staff tour guide is disregarding the right to privacy of a resident whose home you are entering.

Be aware of unsanitary conditions. The nose knows! If you smell urine or feces, or residents look unkempt, with uncombed hair or dirty clothes, this is not the nursing home for you.

After touring the facility, sit in the lobby, go over your notes, and observe the activities around you. If possible, talk with some of the residents and their family members. Get their opinions!

If you like the facility and think it's worth considering, plan to visit again, but at different times and on different days. You may want to check out the facility after business hours or on weekends. You'd be surprised to discover how different some nursing homes operate when the management staff is not typically in the building.

Before you leave, ask the receptionist to see the nursing home survey. Every skilled facility is required to have the latest nursing home survey available. It is usually in a loose-leaf notebook at the desk or posted on a community bulletin board.

VOICE OF EXPERIENCE
Don't Take Every Conversation at Face Value

While looking for a nursing home for Mrs. Taylor, I visited another residence. This was an older building with a more casual feel. Families and friends were sitting in the lobby with their loved ones. It looked very cozy. I struck up a conversation with one of the family members, who raved about the facility.

It took a while before I realized that this woman was not a family member at all, but a personal aide hired by the family to oversee their parent's care. In fact, most of the "visitors" in the lobby were private aides. Besides acknowledging the source of the "raves" I was hearing, I recognized something else that gave me pause about this home. It seemed that many residents had wealthy families who could hire additional help, making me wonder whether they had hired aides because they were unsure the home's care was adequate.

CHAPTER 3

GETTING INTO THE NURSING HOME
OF YOUR CHOICE

You have completed your initial assessment and have narrowed down your list to the leading contenders. Now it's time to turn to getting your loved one into the facility that best suits his or her needs, whether they will be entering from a hospital or from home.

ADMISSION FROM A HOSPITAL

Entry from a hospital is the easiest and most common. Often, after an acute illness, an elderly person will not be strong enough, or physically able, to return to his previous living arrangements. The only prerequisite for nursing home admission is a patient must remain in the hospital for three days. If your loved one goes directly to the nursing home from the hospital, the discharge planner will make all of the arrangements and handle the required pre-admission paperwork upon admission to the nursing home. However, there will be other papers and forms for you to complete that will be discussed later in this chapter.

ADMISSION FROM HOME

Other times– though less frequently – an elderly person is admitted to a nursing home from his or her home. If you are a caregiver applying to a nursing home for your loved one from home, you will have more lead- time, but more responsibility. You must contact each facility yourself and ask about admissions procedures. You will be responsible for coordinating the application and admission process. There is little difference in what you will need to do in either case, but both cases will require a great deal of fast decision-making, so be on your toes.

 *Author's Note*

Whether admitted from hospital or home, be aware that the patient must be seen by her physician within 30 days of applying for admission to a nursing home. If you delay longer than 30 days, you will need to go through the application procedure again.

FIVE "MUST KNOWS" ABOUT
NURSING HOME ADMISSION

This section is primarily for people who have a loved one entering a nursing home from a hospital. These pointers will prepare you for the split-second decisions the hospital may require of you.

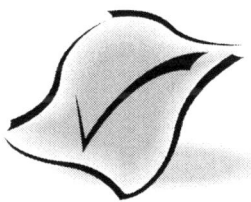

#1: KNOW AT LEAST FIVE PREFERRED NURSING HOMES

Shortly before your loved one is released from the hospital, the discharge planner should give you a written plan that includes the doctor's recommendation for post-hospital care and the expected date of dismissal. Hospitals have strong financial incentives to discharge patients as quickly as possible, so the turnaround time can be as soon as the next day!

The hospital must ask you to name up to five nursing homes that you would like them to contact. If you have done your homework and surveyed the homes in your area, you will be able to do this without any problem. You can pat yourself on the back for being prepared. If you have not investigated nursing homes you will be forced to do some fast footwork and might not be able to make a fully-informed decision.

Hospital discharge planners may be able to offer some suggestions, but they usually rely on information provided by nursing home representatives who visit hospitals. For liability purposes, hospital regulations may also prohibit the discharge planner from offering recommendations.

If you feel your loved one is being dismissed from the hospital too quickly, you can appeal the decision. This will also give you more time to research nursing homes. But all is not lost if events happen too fast for you to plan. If your loved one gets discharged to a facility that you are unhappy with, know that nothing is permanent. You have the freedom of choice. Just start investigating other facilities right away. When you find one that you like with an available bed, let the social worker of that facility know you want to have your loved one transferred. As long as the new facility can meet your loved one's needs, the transition should take only a day or two, and the social worker will do most of the work for you.

 *Author's Note*

In some states, like New York, a patient on Medicaid who no longer needs inpatient hospital care but has not selected a preferred nursing facility can be placed in the first available nursing home bed within 50 miles of his home. You can help avoid this happening to your loved one by having a list of preferred facilities ready.

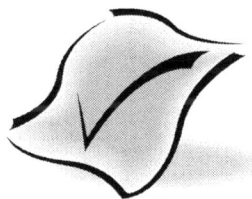

#2: KNOW THE IMPORTANCE OF THE PATIENT EVALUATION FORM

The federal government requires that every prospective resident of a nursing home receive a comprehensive assessment before admission. A patient must meet certain qualifications to be eligible for nursing home acceptance. The assessment is designed to determine the needs of each resident before admittance. The patient must also be screened for mental illness, mental retardation (MR), and developmental disabilities (DDs).

Joanna R. Leefer

New York State's form is called the *Patient Review Instrument (PRI)*. It records a patient's medical history, current condition, and rates the type of care that he will require when entering a nursing home. To view an actual PRI form, visit **www.health.ny.gov/forms/doh-694.pdf.** Other states have similar forms. For example, Ohio's evaluation form is called the *Pre-Admissions Screening Resident Review (PASRR)*.

If a person is diagnosed as having mental illness, retardation, or a developmental disability, they are given a *Level of Care Assessment* as well to determine if they would be better served in a specialized facility. *The Level of Care Assessment* also identifies if the person meets Medicaid criteria for nursing home admission, which determines the appropriate type of long-term care that Medicaid will cover. This form is only needed for seniors receiving Medicaid services.

In some states, there are different procedures for people who pay privately for nursing home care. Patients who pay privately may not have to go through formal assessments, but if their funds run out, the assessments are typically required before Medicaid will be approved. No matter what state or form, be sure to be involved in the evaluation process. You know your loved one's needs better than anyone else.

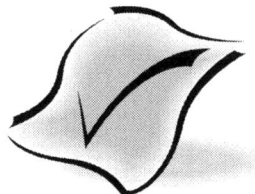

#3: KNOW THAT THERE MAY BE ROOM FOR NEGOTIATION

Nursing home admission decisions are based on many factors: bed availability, care requirements, a patient's condition, etc. A nursing home does not have to provide you with a reason for denial, but sometimes there is room for negotiation. (See Voice of Experience page 54).

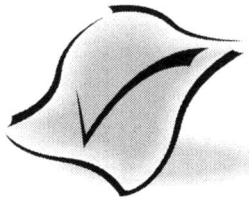

#4: KNOW YOUR FINANCIAL ALTERNATIVES

After nursing home acceptance, the patient is faced with financial decisions. If your loved one is being admitted for short-term rehab, Medicare will pick up most, if not all, of the tab for a period of time. For more information on Medicare, go to the Medicare website at **www.medicare.gov.**

Joanna R. Leefer

Most people are unable to finance the $10,000 - $15,000 a month fee for nursing home care and will need Medicaid assistance. The discharge planner at the hospital or social worker at the nursing home should be able to help.

VOICE OF EXPERIENCE
Consider Your Bargaining Chips

While I was working in advocacy, my agency received a call from a caregiver whose father had dementia. She wanted her dad to be admitted to a particular facility in Brooklyn that had a well-regarded dementia program.

The problem was her dad often became agitated in the evening and the nursing home did not feel it could handle him. After some discussion, the woman asked the facility if they would accept him if his agitation could be contained. The nursing home agreed. The woman had her father's doctor prescribe a mild sedative for the evenings, which helped calm his mood. As a result, he was accepted into the program.

Note: There are arguments for and against the use of sedatives among seniors. In this case, the woman's father was carefully monitored and was not overmedicated.

In another case, a 70-year-old woman with a diagnosis of schizophrenia had been in the hospital due to an accidental overdose of her medication. The family had requested she be placed in the local nursing facility so they could visit often. However, when reviewing the hospital information, the nursing home did not feel they could meet her needs because they did not have a "behavior unit" or "on-site" psychiatric services.

The family really wanted her to be in this particular nursing home, so they visited and spoke to the social worker and the director of nursing. They were able to explain that the behaviors she had exhibited in the hospital were not typical and that family members would be available around the clock to help her settle in, if need be. The facility agreed to take her with the condition that if her needs could not be met she would be transferred immediately. Things worked out fine. The patient worked hard through therapy and was discharged back to her home after rehab.

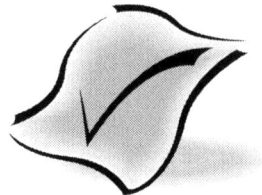

#5: KNOW HOW TO APPEAL A DECISION

Do not settle if you are not happy with the hospital's decision. You can dispute the decision by sending an appeal to *Improving Health Care for the Common Good* (IPRO). The appeal information should be included in the discharge plan.

IPRO is a national not-for-profit organization founded in 1984. It offers a full range of health care assessment services and holds contracts with federal, state, and local government agencies in more than 33 states and the District of Columbia. IPRO will review your appeal and get back to you with a decision. The patient can remain in the hospital, at no cost, until the appeal is reviewed and a decision is made. But work quickly; these appeals are handled promptly. Also, be aware that if your appeal is denied, you may be responsible for any hospital costs incurred during the appeal process. To contact this important organization, or to file a complaint, log onto their website at **http://ipro.org/.** They have a downloadable form that you can file out to file a complaint.

CHAPTER 4

MONITORING CARE: NURSING HOME ADVOCACY

SETTLING IN: NURSING HOME TRANSITION STRATEGIES

Now that your loved one is in a residence, everyone is going to have to adjust to a life change. Your loved one will probably be sharing a room with at least one other person and is going to have much more limited space. Most of the furniture is provided; they will have very little space for personal items: maybe a few photos, some personal items for the bed, and some clothes. This can be upsetting for everyone. Home residents may feel that as if they are losing their autonomy and freedom, and to some extent, they are.

Joanna R. Leefer

I recommend these two important steps to help ease this turbulent transition:

1. VISIT MORE, STAY LONGER. Plan to visit and stay longer than usual during the first two or three weeks to make sure your loved one is adjusting to his or her new home. Many older people get confused before they settle into a routine. Your presence may help calm and comfort them, making the transition easier. It will also give you the chance to make sure your loved ones are getting all the attention they deserve. Your being there will also help the staff adjust their care to the particular needs of the new resident. Your presence will send a message to the staff that you will not accept anything less than great care.

2. LEARN WHO IS IN CHARGE of nursing, social work, and activities, and which aides are responsible for your loved one's day- to-day care. Find out what activities he or she might enjoy. Make sure your loved one is seated with friendly people at meals, and check to see that food requests are being met. This is the time to let your expectations be known. Let the staff know your mom, dad, or spouse is well-loved and deserving of special attention.

VOICE OF EXPERIENCE
Be Sensitive To Your Loved One's Needs

Keep in mind that everyone is different. A loved one may be unhappy about entering a home and may be angry with you for initiating the placement. For example, when you visit your mom, she may become more agitated and may try to make you feel guilty. She might tell you she is unhappy, hoping you will take her home. Speak with the nursing staff to see how she behaves when you are not there. Chances are, she may be just fine when you are not present. If this is the case, you may need to set limits on your visits until she is settled in and is no longer angry.

FOUR POINTERS TO GUARANTEE
GREAT CARE

You have already let the staff know that you will be involved in your loved one's care. Here are four important points that will help you make sure your loved one is safe, happy, and getting the optimal attention.

1. BECOME YOUR LOVED ONE'S HEALTH CARE PROXY

A health care proxy is a legal document that allows an individual to appoint a trusted person to make health care decisions, if one's ability to make decisions is lost. Other states may refer to this document by another name, such as Durable Power of Attorney or Power of Attorney for Health Care. Regardless of the title, these documents allow a patient's wishes to be followed, even when incapable of communicating.

When a person is no longer able to voice his wishes, and there is no documented decision-maker, some states will automatically defer to the next of kin. Other states will require that a guardian be appointed. Often a family member will seek guardianship, but sometimes the court will appoint someone. This person may be a total stranger. So you can see that it is very important to talk with your family members and make sure everyone has a plan in place before the time comes.

A healthcare proxy is a very important document. It offers you legal access to all your loved one's medical records and allows you to make decisions when your loved one is not conscious, even for just a short period of time. This is not to be confused with a living will, which is a written statement of an individual's wishes regarding specific medical treatments.

The health care proxy also allows you to be in the room with your loved one when he is being examined or dressed. This is a very important privilege that I will discuss in more depth in my discussion of pressure sores (page.73). For more information on the health care proxy, see Appendix F.

2. ATTEND THE COMPREHENSIVE CARE PLAN MEETING

Every skilled nursing facility that accepts Medicare or Medicaid funds must develop a care plan for a new resident within the first 21 days after entry. The facility's major decision-makers typically called the Interdisciplinary Team, work together to develop this plan of care. As the name implies, the team consists of members from all disciplines, including nursing, social services, therapy, dietary, activities, and medical.

Nursing home regulations mandate that the family (and resident, if able), must be involved in the CCP. The Interdisciplinary Team will schedule a meeting to review their recommendations, sending written notification and an invitation to family members (and the resident) to attend. While family attendance at this meeting is not mandatory, it is recommended. Remember, your loved one's care will be determined at this time. Important Note: If you are unable to attend at the proposed time, ask for the meeting to be rescheduled. If family members live out of town and cannot attend meetings, their input can be obtained through interviews or phone conversations.

A CCP must be reevaluated at least every three months to determine whether it is still appropriate or whether changes should be made. The plan must also be reassessed if there is a major change in your loved one's condition.

CCP Meeting Pointers

Before the Comprehensive Care Plan meeting, you should compile a list of questions and issues you wish to address. If you are anxious about the meeting, bring a friend or trusted individual, such as a clergyman, for assistance and support. If English is not your first language, you may request an interpreter.

Take notes during the meeting. You might even consider making a recording if that will make you feel more comfortable. Before the meeting ends, review your notes, and make sure all your questions have been answered. Summarize what you feel has been decided and indicate how you feel about the plan.

After the meeting, send a follow-up letter to the primary attendees, thanking them for their time and listing the topics that were discussed and their resolutions. This will ensure that all the people involved have a similar understanding of what transpired. If there are future problems, your letter will serve as a clear record of documented statements.

3. VISIT OFTEN AND VARY YOUR SCHEDULE

You want to make sure your loved one gets the best care at all times, not just when you visit, so be sure to be unpredictable. Don't come at the same time every day. Keep the staff on their toes! Be sure to visit on weekends, evenings, and holidays, when many facilities are not fully staffed. Come at meal times or in the evening to make sure your family member has not been put to bed too early, is not isolated, and is involved in activities. You don't have to stay long, just "pop in" and out. When visiting, introduce yourself to all the staff members, so they know you are watching them. Make sure you let everyone know if you are having doubts about your loved one's care.

If you live in another state or are unable to visit for some reason, you should appoint someone to visit your loved one, either another relative, a friend, or a professional like a geriatric care manager, senior care advisor, or social worker. Make sure you trust the person and feel assured that they will be your eyes, ears, and voice in caring for your loved one.

QUESTIONS TO ASK AT FOLLOW-UP Comprehensive Care Plan Meetings

I mentioned earlier that the Comprehensive Care Plan must be reassessed every three months or whenever there are major changes in the resident's condition. (See #2, page 63). During these meetings be sure you understand how your loved one's condition has changed and what is being done about it. Here are some key questions you should ask during any follow-up meeting.

- What has changed in your loved one's health, behavior, or physical ability and what has caused the change?
- Has the doctor made any changes to the medication?
- Has your loved one's weight changed significantly? If so, why?

- Who is responsible for your loved one's care? Have there been any staff changes, and if so, why?
- Is your loved one participating in activities? (If you think there are any activities your loved one would enjoy, ask if they could be added to the activity schedule.
- Does the staff recommend any particular changes and why?

4. BECOME THE SQUEAKY WHEEL

You know the old adage, "The squeaky wheel gets the grease." You went to all the trouble of investigating a facility that will provide your loved one with the best care, so make sure he or she receives it.

If you are not sure if your mom is being bathed frequently enough, ask. If you think her clothes are wrinkled, let the staff know. Make sure your dad's hair is combed, and that he is well shaven and involved in all the activities he wants to be involved in. The more often you make a comment or ask a question, the more likely the staff will think of you as they are caring for your loved one.

VOICING CONCERNS

Registering your concerns is an art in itself, and communicating them effectively to the proper parties is as important as identifying signs of poor care.

IDENTIFY THE OFFICIAL COMPLAINT CHANNELS

Here are four official channels you can use to ensure that your loved one gets the care he or she desires.

- **The Nursing Home Social Worker:** The social worker is a good place to start when you have a complaint. This person is responsible for maintaining the residents' highest level of physical, mental, and psychosocial well-being and should be able to handle your concerns. Federal law requires all skilled nursing facilities with more than 120 beds to employ at least one full-time social worker with a minimum of a bachelor's degree in social work or "similar professional qualifications." Nursing homes with fewer than 120 beds must still provide social work or social work services, although they do not have to hire a full-time licensed professional.

- **The Nursing Director:** This person is the head of the nursing department. Make sure she has a copy of your loved one's care plan and go over it with her to ensure all the demands are met. If you find any discrepancy in care, make sure the nursing director is informed.

- **Nursing Home Administrator:** In the "chain of command," the administrator is usually the one responsible for the overall operations of the nursing home. In most cases, this person is not a nurse. If the administrator is personally unable to solve your problem, he or she will assign someone to do so.

- **The Nursing Home Ombudsman:** The ombudsman is a professionally trained and certified advocate who helps to resolve nursing home issues on behalf of the residents and their families. The ombudsman is not an employee of the nursing facility, but is trained to help mediate concerns between staff and residents. The Ombudsman Program was first introduced in 1971 as part of an eight- point plan to improve nursing home conditions. In 1978, the program was formally adopted by Congress under the Older Americans Act and established nationwide in all long-term care facilities. In New York State, ombudsmen must participate in a 36-hour training program before they are assigned to a nursing home.

KNOW THE UNOFFICIAL COMPLAINT CHANNELS

In your quest to get the best possible care for your loved one, do not neglect unofficial pathways for registering grievances. Get to know those who are involved in attending to your loved one's day-to-day care including the Certified Nursing Assistants (CNAs) or nurse aides. Activities directors and dining room staff can also be important players in ensuring your loved one's well-being.

Try to be cordial to the staff from the start. They might become your greatest advocates. Many nurse aides do this kind of work because they love it, not just for the paycheck. Acknowledge their good care. Give them a pat on the back, thank them and tell them how good your mom looks, and so forth. While they are not permitted to accept personal gifts, they can usually accept cookies or something that can be shared. It's not a big gesture, but it is a way of showing your appreciation. Often this sign of appreciation will motivate them to do an even better job!

VOICE OF EXPERIENCE
Cordial Relationships Pay Off

In the late stages of my mother's battle with Alzheimer's disease, she lost her ability to balance, became sedentary, and developed pressure (bed) sores. (Note: Pressure sores are often an indication of personal neglect, but in this case, Mom's skin became so fragile, it would tear easily.) The facility ordered a special bed for her that shifted her weight slowly to ensure that she was never resting in one position for long.

One evening I received a whispered call from one of Mom's aides. The aide had noticed that my mother's head sometimes dangled close to the bed railing and she was afraid Mom might choke if the bed shifted too much. The aide told me she had informed the nurse but was afraid they would overlook the seriousness of the situation. The next day, I visited the facility and, without mentioning the aide, told the head nurse that I was concerned about the hazard. I suggested the staff place a bumper around Mom's mattress. They agreed immediately, and the potential threat was averted.

FOUR DANGER SIGNS!

As people age and become more debilitated, some common problems might ring an alarm. Sometimes these issues can be related to poor care, but they can also develop for medical reasons, despite appropriate interventions and care. A very important part of advocacy is recognizing and interpreting these danger signs and making sure interventions are implemented immediately.

#1: SIGNIFICANT WEIGHT LOSS

A sudden loss in weight might be a sign that your loved one is not eating properly. This could indicate that the staff is not watching to see if your family member is able to eat, or is not providing needed assistance. Check to see if there are difficulties with cutting food, handling a fork, or swallowing. Beyond these mechanical difficulties, there are multiple reasons for loss of appetite including depression, medication, mouth or dental pain, infection, or illness. All of these things should be investigated as well.

#2: LETHARGY, SLEEPINESS, MOOD CHANGES

A change in a resident's behavior might be due to a change in medicine or dosage. You should automatically be updated on all changes as they are made. Ask the nurse to review your loved one's medical files to see if there have been adjustments that are not known to you. (This is your right if you are the health care agent for your loved one.) Make sure you are kept informed of all shifts in medications and the reasons for these changes.

#3: UNKEMPT OR UNCLEAN APPEARANCE

Notice your loved one's appearance. The Nursing Home Residents' Bill of Rights states that each person should be clean and well groomed; pay attention to the state of clothing, hair, skin and nails, If your loved one isn't clean, find out why. The staff should not be neglecting a resident.

#4: PRESSURE SORES

One of the greatest dangers in a nursing home is the pressure sore. A pressure sore, also known as a bedsore, is caused by unrelieved pressure, friction, or humidity on a portion of the body, typically over a bony prominence such as the heel, ankle, hips, buttocks, or tailbone. Sometimes a small sore becomes a large wound that can become infected and, in extreme cases, cause death. If your loved one is unable to turn or reposition independently, there should be a care plan in place to help prevent pressure areas. (Those who are able to get up and down without assistance are less likely to develop pressure areas.) (See page 73 for more information on Pressure Sores)

Nursing home aides are responsible for checking for infection or sores, but even a conscientious aide may miss the signs. The best method to determine if your loved one is developing a pressure sore is to physically check. Stay in the room while the aide is dressing, bathing, or changing your loved one. Many families feel this is an infringement of a loved one's personal space, but it is an important duty. If you are a family member or the health care agent, you are entitled to stay even if the staff member suggests that you leave. If you are not a family member but you are responsible for an individual's care, make sure you are assigned a health care proxy. (See Appendix F.)

PRESSURE SORES:
SYMPTOMS AND TREATMENT

Pressure sores are a very serious problem among the elderly. If they are not treated quickly they can cause severe complications or even death. The sores are categorized in four stages.

Symptoms at each state include:

Stage 1 - The skin becomes inflamed and could be itchy. The skin is not broken or open, but will look red and could feel warm when touched.

Stage 2 - The deeper layers of skin will be more extensively damaged. The skin may blister or become an open sore. The skin around the wound may become discolored, and the area around the sore will be very painful.

Stage 3 - The pressure sore will become an ulcer and the wound will look like a crater. This is very dangerous as it may leave tissues seriously damaged.

Stage 4 - This is the most serious pressure sore stage. The skin and tissue are severely damaged, causing a large wound. Muscles, bones, tendons, and joints can be affected at this stage. Infection can occur, and can spread to the blood, heart, and bone, resulting in amputations or death. Some signs that infection from a pressure sore has spread include fever, chills, mental confusion, rapid heartbeat, and weakness.

HOW TO PREVENT A PRESSURE SORE

The best way to prevent a pressure sore is to change the patient's position every few hours if the patient is confined to a bed. Innovative equipment such as specially designed chair cushions, bed covers, and pillows have been developed to help alleviate the problem. Special new beds can be programmed to continually shift the patient so that no body part sustains continuous pressure.

HOW TO TREAT A PRESSURE SORE

The treatment for a pressure sore depends on its severity. If the sore is discovered in the earliest stage, an antibiotic ointment can be used. If deeper tissue is infected, stronger antibiotics will be necessary.

HOW TO COMPLAIN: BE POLITE, BE PROFESSIONAL

KEEP A RECORD

If you are concerned about some part of your loved one's care, be sure to document your concerns in writing. Start with the date and time, what your concern is, where it took place, and who was involved. Continue to create a record whenever you see something questionable. Also cite any conversations that you had with staff regarding any issues. You will now be armed with a written record showing names, dates, times, and events, which will help the management staff investigate and solve problems.

TALK TO THE APPROPRIATE PERSON

Most people want to do their jobs well, so a lapse may merely be an oversight. With this in mind, my first suggestion would be to talk with the responsible person about your concerns.

The best way to approach staff members is to assume they are professional. Talk with them pleasantly, but firmly. Don't yell or appear confrontational. No matter how right you are, people do not respond well to accusations. If you attack, they will probably become defensive and return the attack, escalating the situation. Even if you get the desired change in behavior, you will lose your allies. On the other hand, you don't want to be too conciliatory. You are both adults with a problem that can be solved if you discuss it and come up with a solution.

If all goes as planned, your problem will be resolved. If you feel you have not reached a satisfactory solution, take the next step and make an appointment with the head of the department. For example, if you have a concern about care issues, schedule an appointment with the head of nursing. If it is a dietary concern, ask to speak with the dietician or dietary manager, and so forth.

 *Important Note:*

Do not bribe nursing home staff! Bribing is against the law

Bring your diary to any meetings you have Explain the situation, express your concerns, and ask for resolution. After you leave, send a formal thank you to the person in charge, expressing your appreciation for the meeting, indicating the steps you both agreed to take, and asking to be kept informed of the action. You should also mention a date by which you expect the situation to be resolved.

These actions are generally effective, but if not, ask to speak with the nursing home administrator, and go through the following steps:

- Request an appointment
- Express your concerns

- Show your log

- Describe the actions you have already taken

- Ask for resolution

It is always best to try to first try to solve problems with the nursing home staff. But if you are not satisfied with the results, the nursing home ombudsman may be able to help. The ombudsman is trained to resolve nursing home issues on behalf of the residents and their families. The last resort is to file a formal complaint with the Department of Health. You can do this anonymously if you are not comfortable giving your name. This should be done only if you have a serious concern, have exhausted all other avenues, and have received no satisfaction. Once a complaint is registered with the Department of Health, it will be indicated on the nursing home's survey report.

TO FILE, OR NOT TO FILE, A COMPLAINT?

There are arguments for and against filing a formal complaint with the state. When you file a complaint, either over the phone or via a website, you will receive a file number and will be kept informed of the status of the investigation. If you want to follow up before the process ends, you can give your number to receive a status reports on the complaint.

Joanna R. Leefer

Some family members are afraid to mention their names when filing a complaint because they are concerned that the home will retaliate against their loved one. While the investigating team is not permitted to reveal who actually filed the complaint, a savvy nursing-home staff will likely be able to figure this out by the questions the team asks or the information they request. In theory, the nursing home cannot retaliate against a resident – or his or her family -- for complaining, but many families are concerned nonetheless.

The other option is to file a complaint anonymously. But know that if you do not give your name, the operator cannot give you a complaint number, making it impossible to learn what is being done.

 *Important Note:*
Sometimes actions speak louder than words. If you have reached the point where you feel your only recourse is to take official action, you must consider the possibility that your loved one is in an unsafe facility. I recommend transferring your loved one to another facility, then filing a formal complaint.

AVOIDING NURSING HOME-RELATED NIGHTMARES

Moving into a skilled nursing home can be a traumatic experience for both you and your loved one. Once settled in, there are still many unanswered questions that can haunt the all parties. Here are four potential troubling scenarios that can arise and how you can handle them.

NIGHTMARE #1: THE STAY-AT-HOME SPOUSE HAS FINANCIAL CHALLENGES

A big concern for many older couples arises when one spouse must go into a nursing home and the other stays at home. How will the stay-at-home spouse survive financially if the nursing home spouse must register for Medicaid?

Fortunately, in September 1989, the U.S. Congress passed the Impoverishment Prevention Provision, which allows the stay-at-home spouse, also called the "community spouse" to receive a Community Spouse Resource Allowance (CSRA) and a Minimum Monthly

79

Joanna R. Leefer

Maintenance Needs Allowance (MMMNA) to keep him or her from depleting all the couple's financial resources.

The Community Spousal Resource Allowance is approximately 50% of joint income at the time the spouse enters the nursing home, but this varies from state to state. Check with an elder law attorney to get more information on your state's regulations. For more information on federal and state government, log on to www.medicaid.gov and type "Spousal Impoverishment" in the search category.

Some states such as New York, Florida and Connecticut provide more generous options called the "Spousal Refusal" provision. Spousal Refusal permits the institutionalized spouse to shift excess assets into the name of the community spouse. The community spouse then signs and files a document with the Department of Social Services (DSS), indicating that she refuses to contribute any of this income to the ill spouse.

In New York State in 2012, the maximum income the "well" spouse was permitted to keep was $3,000 per month of the couple's combined income and $100,000 of all "resources" or assets. Other exempt assets include a home and one automobile. For more information on protecting your family's financial situation, contact an elder law attorney.

NIGHTMARE #2: INVOLUNTARY TRANSFERS OR DISCHARGES

Nothing can be more frightening than the thought of a resident being arbitrarily transferred from one nursing home to another. Fortunately, this rarely occurs. A nursing home can transfer or discharge a resident under only five conditions:

- The resident's medical care has changed, and the home can no longer provide the proper treatment.

- The resident no longer needs nursing home care because his condition has improved.

- The resident is endangering herself or other individuals.

- If paying privately for care, the resident has not paid for care for at   least 15 days.

- The nursing home plans to close.

(Source: The Nursing Home Reform Law of 1987)

Know that, in all cases, the family must receive a written note at least 30 days before this change. (This requirement is waived if the resident is: endangering himself or another resident, needs urgent medical care, or has requested the discharge). The written notice must include one of the following:

- The reason for the transfer or discharge
- The date of the requested change
- The location where the resident is being transferred

The discharge notice must also include information on how and where to appeal the decision and in what time frame. Families can file an appeal and request a hearing within 20 days of receiving this notice.

If you file an appeal during this period, the nursing home cannot transfer the resident until after the appeal is heard and a written decision is determined. (See appealing a hospital decision, page 56).

NIGHTMARE #3: HOSPITAL STAYS & NURSING HOME READMISSION

What happens if a resident needs temporary hospital care? Each state has different bed-hold policies, but the federal law guarantees every nursing home resident who must be hospitalized will get an available bed in a shared room when he returns, although not necessarily the same bed as before. The law also requires that each nursing home provide the resident with the state's specific policy. Be sure to know your state's policy. In 2011–12, California had a seven-day-bed hold policy; after which, a resident had to take the first available bed. In 2012, New York held a nursing bed for 14 days per year.

NIGHTMARE #4: INVOLUNTARY ROOM TRANSFERS

Be aware that a Skilled Nursing Facility (SNF) that receives Medicare or Medicaid funding must give a resident advance notice before the room or roommate of the resident is changed within the facility. The home should also explain why the change is necessary. The Medicare and Medicaid rules do not specify how much advance notice is required.

CHAPTER 5

ALZHEIMER'S/DEMENTIA CARE

Almost every nursing home and assisted living facility has a "Dementia/Alzheimer's" program, but beware, not all dementia programs offer the same quality of care. Alzheimer's disease is the best-known form of dementia, but this condition spans a broad range of diagnoses and symptoms. Other forms of dementia include vascular dementia, dementia with Lewy bodies, frontal temporal dementia, Parkinson's disease, as well as approximately 50 lesser-known varieties. Each of these types of dementia displays various symptoms and affects functional and cognitive abilities in distinct ways, requiring specialized treatment. For this reason, it is important to understand your loved one's condition when evaluating a home placement.

There are several specific concerns you must consider when evaluating a dementia ward. Would you prefer that your loved one live on a floor with residents who do not have dementia? Do you want them in a locked ward, or one that attaches wander guards to each resident? Would you like them to have access to tailored programs for dementia patients? How do you feel about giving sedatives or other psychoactive medications to your loved one? I will address some major considerations below.

LIVING TOGETHER OR APART

Some facilities feel that dementia patients should live alongside other patients rather than be isolated among themselves. They believe that living with less mentally impaired individuals offers more stimuli than can be found in a separate unit. Many dementia patients are able to participate with higher-functioning residents and enjoy the mainstream activities in a home. In fact, non-Alzheimer's residents often enjoy helping dementia patients and take them under their wing, providing a friend and advocate for those who are more impaired.

Other facilities feel that dementia patients require a special environment. People with dementia can become agitated by the noises that abound in a traditional care unit, as their brains don't know how to sort out and process sounds. As a result, they may begin to act out. (Over-stimulation can be just as bad as under-stimulation for a person with cognitive impairments.) For this reason, dementia units are typically kept quieter and more serene than standard care units.

Moreover, people with dementia can be disruptive to other residents. As illustrated by my own experience outlined below, they sometimes wander into other patients' rooms and act out inappropriately. Clearly, you will need to make your own decisions on issues like this.

VOICE OF EXPERIENCE
Some Behavior is up to Interpretation

In the facility where my mother stayed, many of the dementia residents on her floor would often make their way into other residents' rooms and rummage through their closets and drawers. Frequently, I would meet my mother in the dining room and notice her clothes on another resident, or find my mother wearing someone else's outfit. This never bothered me—I felt it made the floor more "family-like" and gave the unit a feeling of camaraderie. But some families did not feel as kindly toward this type of behavior,

DEMENTIA AND DRUGS

There has been a growing controversy over the use of sedatives and anti-psychotic medication for Alzheimer's patients. Many patients in the early and middle stages of the disease become restless, aggressive, delusional and do not sleep through the night. Some facilities encourage the use of sedatives to calm aggressive behavior. This is fine if it makes the resident more comfortable. But there is a thin line between what the resident truly needs and what is being administered to make the staff's duties easier.

Agitation can be triggered by factors like pain, anxiety, hunger, or the need to toilet. Before assuming that sedatives are the only solution, a doctor should assess any possible underlying factors that might be triggering or aggravating a patient's symptoms. Sometimes there are simple solutions such as soothing the individual by sitting with him or her for a while, or distracting them with an activity such as listening to music, chatting, or a hand massage. Such non-drug treatments are often as effective as medication and leave no aftereffects.

ACTIVITIES FOR STAGES OF ALZHEIMER'S DISEASE

Alzheimer's Disease is the most common form of dementia, so I will focus on this condition and provide pointers on what to look for when accessing activity programs. Alzheimer's Disease gets progressively worse over time and each phase of this disease requires a different type of treatment and activity. Outlined below are the major symptoms of each disease stage along with the types of activities that are most appropriate for each level.

Early stage — The symptoms in the early stages of Alzheimer's include difficulty with short-term memory, poor attention span, trouble organizing, inability to follow complex instructions, and forgetting how things work (e.g. a washing machine or microwave).

Many individuals with early Alzheimer's are still relatively social and can pass for "normal." Motor and physical skills are still good and these patients can do rudimentary activities such as laundry and cleaning. People at this stage need room to walk around and require activities that involve motor skills and brain stimulation. They can be kept active through walking, dancing, simple exercise, and even some baking – as long as someone is watching the oven.

Middle stage — Symptoms at this stage include difficulty with both short and long-term memory. Patients can wander and get lost; they might resist dressing and bathing, lose inhibitions, experience hallucinations, and may not recognize their own reflection in the mirror. They might also experience difficulty with complex motor skills such as handling a fork or knife.

Activities appropriate for individuals in this group are more simplified and involve remembrances and sensory stimulation. Programs can include simple jigsaw puzzles with less than 10 pieces, sorting activities such as with buttons, coins, or beans. Listening to familiar music and looking at scrapbooks that elicit memories are other recommended pastimes.

Late stage —Symptoms at this phase include severely diminished cognitive and physical functioning, including difficulty engaging, talking in gibberish, loss of ability to balance and walk, and trouble eating and swallowing.

Activities are primarily concentrated on sensory exercises such as identifying colorful objects or listening to music or stories told by others. People at this stage are particularly receptive to hand massage, calming sounds, scents of flowers or spices, and touching of different textured items, such as soft toys, rope, and knobby or silky fabrics. To maintain the person's range of joint motion, it is helpful to carefully and slowly move his or her arms and legs two to three times a day. They may also benefit from less- strenuous physical activities like tossing a ball.

FINAL STAGES—COMFORT CARE

A growing number of residential care facilities are adopting a new late stage Alzheimer's disease treatment approach called comfort care. This approach emphasizes the emotional needs of the Alzheimer's patient and provides palliative care to ease discomfort, sometimes through the use of heavy painkillers.

This new practice acknowledges that people with Alzheimer's disease will not get better and should therefore be given as much comfort and leeway as possible, including freedom to eat, sleep and dress as they wish. The initiative also advocates pain management, recognizing that most violent and disruptive behavior in Alzheimer's patients stems from their inability to express discomfort or pain.

The concept of comfort care was devised by the Beatrice Campus in Phoenix, Arizona. Their program called Comfort First set the stage for similar programs throughout the country. The New York City Chapter of the Alzheimer's Association has adopted the Comfort First model and is introducing the program in select nursing home facilities in New York City and Brooklyn. To learn more about this program and where it is being introduced, contact your local Alzheimer's Association Chapter at **http://www.alz.org/**

HOW TO EVALUATE A DEMENTIA UNIT

Now that I've introduced you to many of the important issues to consider when evaluating a dementia unit, touring is the next critical step in selecting a facility for your loved one. Do not assume that just because you like other sections of a nursing facility the dementia section will also be acceptable. Many facilities are not well-trained in dementia or Alzheimer's care and are often less sensitive to the needs of patients with such diagnoses.

When looking at a skilled nursing home's dementia services, make sure to consider your loved one's current and future needs. Remember that Alzheimer's disease is a progressive condition, and your loved one's requirements will change as his or her condition deteriorates.

SIX CRUCIAL QUESTIONS TO ASK:

1. **Is the dementia ward large enough so your loved one will not feel confined?** Ask how much space the residents have to live in. If your loved one is active, make sure the facility has enough room in which to walk around safely.

2. **Are the activities appropriate for your loved one's intellectual capabilities?** Remember that people in the early stages of Alzheimer's need more stimulation and more challenging activities than those in the later stages. Ask about the types of activities that are available for each stage. (see page 88).

3. **Does the dementia ward provide a positive environment?** Many dementia floors include large murals on the walls that provide colorful scenes or images. Make sure these murals are not disturbing or confusing to someone with cognitive impairment.

4. **Are music and singing included in the activities?** Studies show that music has a beneficial impact on dementia patients. According to scientific reports, music resides in a different part of the brain than basic thinking and is not affected in the same way. Many residents

with advanced dementia still sing or play musical instruments, even if they can no longer express themselves in other ways.

5. **Is the staff trained to handle dementia and Alzheimer's patients?** People with dementia often go through a period in the evening called "sun downing," a time when they become more confused and agitated. Ask the staff how they handle residents who act out during different times of the day.

6. **Are the residents kept clean, well dressed, and treated with the same respect as any other patient in the facility?** A checklist can be a helpful tool in evaluating a nursing home's Alzheimer or dementia unit when you visit.

Evaluating a Nursing Home's Alzheimer or Dementia Unit			
Dementia Ward	Facility A	Facility B	FacilityC
Separate floor			
Separate unit			
Safety measures for residents			
Wander guards			
Locked floor			
Types of activities			
Trained staff			

Joanna R. Leefer

VOICE OF EXPERIENCE
Take My Advice—All Dementia Care Is NOT Created Equal

When my mother was in the early stages of Alzheimer's, she was still very physically active. We found a nursing facility with an Alzheimer's program that seemed to meet her needs. To ensure safety, each resident was given a wander guard (a bracelet that sets off alarms if the person leaves the designed area). The Alzheimer's program was in a large, well-lit room and included activities such as cooking, singing, watching TV, and interacting with the staff. Unfortunately, my mother wasn't interested in sitting. Her attention span was very short, so she continually wandered out of the room and set off all the alarms. Staff members were constantly running after her to bring her back into the room.

After a few days, my family was called into the administrator's office and informed that our mother did not fit the program's model and she would have to either leave or be placed in the nursing home unit.

We realized that Mom needed much more space. With this in mind, we found a facility that had a separate floor for Alzheimer's patients, where she would be able to walk around to her heart's content, day and night. In addition, this facility had programs and activities for all stages of dementia, ranging from folding towels and sheets, to physical exercises and activities, to more sedentary programs such as working with crayons or moving colorful objects, for those with advanced disease.

CHAPTER 6

THE NURSING HOME
REHABILITATION UNIT

Some acute-care hospitals have rehabilitation (rehab) units that require patients to do several hours of intensive therapy daily. Elderly people typically cannot tolerate this level of activity, so short- term – or sub-acute-- rehab in a skilled nursing facility can be just the ticket.

These units specialize in providing care for elderly people who have had an acute illness or injury (such as a stroke, pneumonia, cardiac issues, fractures, joint replacements, or other surgeries) and are too weak to return to their previous living arrangements. A geriatrician once told me that for every day an elderly person lies in a hospital bed, it will take approximately one week of therapy to get him back to his prior level of function. So, for those in the hospital for five days, it will take approximately five weeks of therapy (of course it may take much longer if they have had a stroke).

Rehabilitation in a skilled nursing facility is a team effort, involving the physician; physical, occupational, or speech therapists; and skilled nursing services. Physical therapy (PT) usually deals with the lower part of the body (legs). PTs will work on balance, walking, and transferring from one surface to another. Occupational therapy (OT) works on the upper body (hands and arms) and tasks such as buttoning clothes, bathing, combing hair, cooking, writing, etc. Speech therapy (ST) in a nursing home focuses on swallowing issues more often than talking issues. Like other muscles, those used in swallowing can weaken and put people at risk for aspiration and pneumonia. Typically, an RN will check the patient during every shift, monitoring vital signs and doing a thorough head-to-toe assessment, while focusing on the body system related to the acute illness (e.g., respiratory assessment for pneumonia, neurological assessment for a stroke). The physician will be notified if any abnormalities are discovered.

EVALUATING A
REHABILITATION FACILITY

Use the same basic evaluation criteria for a short-term care facility that you would for a long-term institution. As before, you will be concerned with proximity, safety, cleanliness, privacy, and food, but now your major emphasis should be on the rehabilitation department. When you tour the facility, make sure to see where the rehabilitation room or "therapy gym" is located, the size of the room, the type of equipment, and the ratio of staff members to patients. Be particularly sensitive to where the equipment is located. Is it in the basement or in a sunny section of the building? Environment is important. If the room is dank and dark, people feel less motivated.

If your loved one is physically able to use the exercise equipment, check it out. What is the state of the equipment? Is it modern? If your loved one is too weak, frail, or cognitively impaired to use equipment safely, ask the therapist how they will proceed with rehab. Notice the interaction between the staff and the patients. Are they attentive? Encouraging? Or do they stand back and leave the patients to pretty much fend for themselves?

Evaluating a Rehabilitation Facility			
Rehab	Facility A	Facility B	Facility C
Types of Equipment			
Attention from Staff			
Space for Equipment			

FINANCING REHAB

Medicare Part A pays for short-term rehabilitation. Under traditional Medicare, a patient must be admitted to a hospital for at least three consecutive nights to qualify, but some Medicare HMOs have different criteria. Once admitted to the nursing home, patients are evaluated for individual rehab needs and the estimated number of days needed to reach their goals. Medicare will determine if the person qualifies for care.

Traditional Medicare will pay the total cost of rehab, minus doctor's bills, for the first 20 days. Beginning on Day 21, traditional Medicare will continue to pay approximately 80% of the cost of treatment for the remainder of the time up to 100 days. A supplemental insurance plan, Medicaid, long-term care insurance, or the patient must pick up the remaining cost. After 100 days, the patient is no longer covered by traditional Medicare Part A. Medicare HMO plans are all different. Some pay 100% for the entire stay, some have co-pays, some are limited to 100-day benefit periods, whereas others cover patients (as long as they meet the criteria) up to an entire year. Be aware that although this time may be "available" to the patient, it is not guaranteed. The patient must meet criteria and make progress toward goals.

TWO STEPS FOR GETTING GREAT REHAB

Step #1: Advocating for a loved one who is in a rehabilitation wing is very similar to advocating for a person in a long-term care situation. The staff will assess your loved one and finalize a treatment plan within two days of being admitted to a nursing home. After the initial assessment, the team will schedule a care plan meeting with you. They will discuss the plan for rehabilitation and may give an estimate of how long they expect rehab to continue.

As with the Comprehensive Care Plan (CCP) meeting, (page 65) it is important that you prepare for this meeting by writing down a list of issues you want to address. Take notes, and bring a companion with you if you feel another set of eyes and ears could be useful during the meeting. Be certain to let all concerned know your loved one's prior level of functioning was, and what he or she needs to return home, such as the ability to climb steps, make simple meals, manage medications, etc. This will help individualize the treatment plan.

Make sure you agree with the plan. Some facilities offer "home treatments" in which the person is taken home for an hour or so and put through activities of his daily routine. This is very helpful because each person's home is different, and any problem can be identified and worked on before discharge. If you think this would be beneficial, ask the staff about this option.

Visit as often as you can. You may want to observe some therapy treatments to make sure your loved one is participating and making progress. Sometimes people do better when family members are present; sometimes they don't. So if you are in doubt about how your presence affects your loved one, ask the therapists. Make sure you stay involved and are informed of the progress so that you aren't surprised when discharge plans are made.

VOICE OF EXPERIENCE
Know When To Say No!

During my father's stay at an assisted living facility, he was prescribed an anti-depression medication that affected his balance. After some dangerous falls, he was hospitalized until the side effects wore off and was prescribed a new medication. However, after five weeks in the hospital, my dad's legs became so weak that he could not walk by himself, so he went into rehab at a nursing home. Physical and occupational therapists evaluated him, and a treatment plan was implemented that included 20 minutes of exercise twice a day. After four weeks, the staff declared he had reached a plateau in his progress and recommended discharge.

My family was not satisfied with this decision. My father performed with a therapy team twice a day for 20 minutes as planned, but the rest of the day he remained in his wheelchair. I argued that it was hard for my father to regain his strength with only 40 minutes of exercise daily and suggested that an aide be assigned to him during the day to help him walk to and from the dining room and the bathroom. The staff agreed, and my father was allocated another three weeks of rehab.

Although he never achieved his former level of activity, Dad was able to reach a more satisfactory level of strength and function.

Step #2: As discussed above, Medicare may not pay for the total 100-day stay. Once the rehabilitation staff and/or Medicare determine the person is no longer benefiting from treatment (or no longer making progress), Medicare will cease payment. If you don't agree with this decision and believe your loved one can still make progress, you may appeal this decision. Make sure you have valid reasons for believing that your loved one should continue treatment. Follow the instructions on the back of the Medicare denial note and file an appeal. The case manager in the nursing home should be able to help you with this.

NEW ADVOCACY INFORMATION
ON REHAB THERAPY!

On January 24, 2013 a new ruling modified the standards for continuing physical, occupational or speech therapy to patients' advantage. Prior to 2013 Medicare determined that therapy payments could be curtailed prior to 100 days if a patient "plateaued", i.e. stopped improving in their treatment. On January 24, 2013, that determination was revised based on a ruling by the U. S. District Court for the District of Vermont in the case of Jimmo v. Sebelius. As of that date, a patient's therapy can continue as long as it will prevent or slow an individual's deterioration and "...maintain a beneficiary at the maximum practicable level of function." That means that a patient need not exhibit improvement to continue rehab. Rather, rehab should continue if the treatment helps the patient maintain an optimum level of performance. This is a big plus for patients, supporting the belief those patients often need therapy just to maintain their current level of performance.

This new ruling does not mean that a patient can continue to receive physical, occupational or speech therapy indefinitely. There is still a 100-day cut- off date. But it does entitle you to appeal a therapy termination decision if you feel your loved one can still benefit from the therapy even if she is no long progressing.

The decision on the Jimmo v. Sebelius case has not been well publicized. Even many professionals are not aware of the change.

To read more about it go to:

http://www.cms.gov/Medicare/Medicare-Fee-for-Service-Payment/SNFPPS/Downloads/Jimmo-FactSheet.pdf

Epilogue

If you have read this book, chances are you have embarked on a noble yet scary journey. Finding the right nursing home for a relative or friend is a daunting task. The process of ensuring that a loved one gets the best care can feel impossible. After all, when you think about it, you are making a major life decision for another person: planning the next phase of someone's life. I hope the tips in this book will assist you and help you transport your loved one toward a new beginning in a safe environment that will ultimately make him or her feel as if they are "almost home."

Please keep me informed of your progress. I'd welcome any stories or new information on your experiences. If you have any questions or comments, send them to me at **jleefer@gmail.com.** Also follow me on my blog at **www.joannaleefer.com.** I will continue to update you on new developments in nursing home care and other types of care that will help you in the future.

APPENDICES

Appendix A

EARLY NURSING HOME FACILITIES

In the early- and mid-twentieth century, a nursing home could be a menacing place. Most people have heard tales of mistreatment and neglect. New Yorkers, for example, may recall Bernard Bergman, who was involved in a huge nursing home scandal in the early 1970s. Investigators exposed the extreme neglect of residents living in the Tower Nursing Home that Bergman owned in Manhattan. Witnesses claimed that residents suffered from neglect, bedsores, dehydration, and malnutrition. The Tower Nursing Home was forced to close in 1974. Bergman was brought to trial and eventually sentenced to prison.

This scandal, along with other cases throughout the country, brought to light the need for more regulations of nursing homes. In 1987, President Ronald Reagan signed into law the first major revision of federal standards that covered nursing home care since the creation of Medicare and Medicaid in 1962. This legislation, called the Federal Nursing Home Reform Act of 1987, provided guidelines for acceptable and expected care in nursing homes and other long-term care facilities.

In addition, the act established greater supervision and regulations for facilities that requested Medicare or Medicaid funding.

This new legislation contained a set of regulations that defined minimum standards of care and defined the rights for people living in certified nursing facilities. These standards also set the groundwork for any future advocacy work, such as your plan for ensuring your loved one's care.

Some of these standards are expressed in every state's Nursing Home Residents' Bill of Rights. A resident has the right to:

- A quality of life and quality of care in any nursing facility that accepts Medicare/Medicaid.
- A right to be discharged or transferred from a nursing home only if there is a medical reason, or if his welfare or the welfare of others are endangered, or for nonpayment.
- A right to be free of any physical or chemical restraints imposed for purposes of discipline or for the convenience of the staff. Restraints may not be used except under the

direction of a physician and only to treat medical symptoms.

- A right to take part in appropriate activities and engage in social, religious, and community activities of choice. Note: There are many more rights that will be discussed in greater depth in the section on nursing home advocacy.

Appendix B

INSTITUTIONAL MEDICAID

The Institutional Medicaid program is a joint federal and state program that finances lower-income people who need skilled nursing home care. To be eligible for institutional Medicaid, an elderly person must:

- Be 65 or older or disabled as determined by Social Security criteria
- Be a U.S. citizen or qualified non-citizen
- Must fall below a predetermined federal/state income and asset level

There are two ways to qualify for Institutional Medicaid.

Your loved one's monthly gross income (job income, wages, and other income) and asset level is less than a predetermined federal and state limit. Each state level is different but must fall below the federal government's definition of "poverty level."

Your loved one may transfer additional income or assets to obtain eligibility. However, this transfer must be five years before your loved one needs nursing home care. This five-year requirement is called the "look back" period. A person may still receive skilled nursing care before that period is reached, but there will be a stiff monetary penalty.

It is best to consult an elder law attorney to determine your loved one's eligibility requirements and if there are some incomes and assets that might be exempt. Every state has its own individual income/asset requirement. To find out your state's Medicaid requirement, contact your state's Medicaid department or search the Internet under your state and "Institutional Medicaid," e.g., "Institutional Medicaid + North Carolina."

The 2013 Medicaid eligibility requirements for New York State are listed below.

	Income	Assets
One-Person Household	$800*	$14,000
Two-Person Household	$1,175*	$21,150

Appendix C

HOW TO READ
A NURSING HOME SURVEY

A nursing home survey will look confusing, but here are some tips that will make it more manageable.

The investigative team rates each deficiency on a severity and frequency level rating from Level A (least dangerous) through Level L (extremely dangerous).

The following grid shows how deficiencies are cited by scope and severity:

SEVERITY	SCOPE		
	(Column 1) Isolated	(Column 2) Pattern	(Column 3) Wide-spread
(Row 4) Immediate jeopardy to resident health or safety	J	K	L
(Row 3) Actual harm that is not immediate jeopardy	G	H	I
(Row 2) No actual harm with potential for more than minimal harm that is not immediate jeopardy	D	E	F
(Row 1) No actual harm with potential for minimal negative impact	A	B	C

Source: *Centers for Medicare & Medicaid Services*

The columns represent the scope or how many residents are affected.

- Column 1: Isolated. This indicates a very small number of residents are affected or that the situation occurred only occasionally.

- Column 2: Pattern. This indicates that more than a few residents are affected, and more than a limited number of staff members are involved.

- Column 3: Widespread. This signifies that the problem affects more than 75% of all residents or constitutes a systemic failure in a facility (or that the system of practice is completely broken). The rows represent the severity or seriousness of the deficiency issue or its associated potential for harm.

- Row 1: Letters A, B, and C – Potential for minimal harm. This means the deficiencies not serious but may negatively affect the resident. There is no actual harm. An example: the nursing home's statement of deficiencies was not posted, or the nursing home did not have a properly installed a fire-alarm system.

- Row 2: D, E, and F – Minimal harm or potential for actual harm. This indicates that a resident or residents were caused some minimal discomfort due to a minor infringement of a regulation. An example would be a staff member served food with improperly washed hands but no one became infected.

- Row 3: G, H, and I – Actual harm. This indicates a resident was negatively affected by an infringement. An example: a resident falls asleep while smoking in bed and a fire results, causing the resident to suffer smoke-inhalation injuries. Level G and higher classifications typically indicate serious problems. This is a warning sign. Reconsider this facility or find out if this problem has been rectified and is unlikely to reoccur.

- Row 4: J, K, and L – Immediate jeopardy. These are the worst tags a facility can get. These tags indicate a resident was seriously injured or died because of an infraction of the regulation. An example: a resident with dementia was found outside the facility heading toward a busy street with no staff assistance. Immediate corrective action is necessary when this deficiency is identified. These violations usually come with big fines. In New York, the maximum fine allowed under law is $2,000 per violation. Keep in mind that these scenarios are examples. Many factors could change the scope and severity of the citation. Each survey team is different.

Appendix D

NURSING HOME CHECKLIST

Nursing Home Checklist

	Nursing Home #1	Nursing Home #2	Nursing Home #3
Quality of Life			
Is the room spacious or cramped?			
Is there space for personal items?			
Are the rooms well-lit and a comfortable temperature?			
Do the rooms smell and look clean?			
Is there an outside sitting area and is it pleasant?			
Are there spaces where guests can visit privately?			
Is the staff courteous and attentive?			
Quality of Care			
Do residents look well groomed, clothes are clean, and their hair is combed?			
Is there enough staff for resident care?			
Do residents appear alert, occupied and content?			
Are aides assigned to particular rooms?			

Nursing Home Checklist	Nursing Home #1	Nursing Home #2	Nursing Home #3
Safety			
Are there handrails in the hall?			
Are any residents left unattended in dangerous situations?			
Note any safety features for getting in and out of bed, i.e., assit rairs or grab bars.			
Is there an evacuation plan posted on the wall?			
Are the halls uncluttered?			
Can residents easily ring for assistance when they are in bed?			
Is there security in the lobby?			
Nutrition and Hydration			
Is there a weekly menu posted?			
Is there a variety of food offering?			
Are aides available for residents who need assistance eating?			
Are meals served at the proper temperature?			
Do residents have easy access to water?			

Appendix E

FEDERAL NURSING HOME RESIDENTS' BILL OF RIGHTS

Under federal regulations, all nursing homes are required by law to have written policies called the Nursing Home Residents' Bill of Rights. These policies describe the rights of the residents. Nursing homes are required by law to make these policies available to any resident who requests them.

State laws for nursing home care usually mirror federal counterparts because the traditional standard of care for the nursing home industry is based on federal law. A violation of a state nursing home code should also be a violation of federal laws. If a nursing home is qualified under Medicare, the applicable governing statutes should be federal statutes.

Joanna R. Leefer

The Nursing Home Residents' Bill of Rights should include and define (but not be limited to) the following rights:

The right to be informed of your rights and the policies of the home

The right to be informed about the facility's services and charges

The right to be informed about your medical condition and treatment

The right to participate in planning your care and medical treatment

The right to choose your own physician

The right to manage personal finances

The right to privacy, dignity, and respect

The right to personal possessions

The right to be free from abuse and restraints

The right to voice grievance without retaliation

The right to be discharged or transferred only for medical reasons

The rights to access to any visitors

To locate a particular state's Bill of Rights, go to the Internet and search for "Nursing Home Residents' Bill of Rights" and the state.

Appendix F

THE HEALTH CARE PROXY

WHAT IS A HEALTH CARE PROXY?

A health care proxy is a legal document that allows you to appoint someone you trust to make health care decisions for you if you lose the ability to make decisions for yourself. Other states may refer to this document by another name, such as Durable Power of Attorney or Power of Attorney for Health Care. Regardless of the title, these documents allow a patient's wishes to be followed even when she is incapable of communicating.

When a person is no longer able to voice her wishes, and there is no documented decision-maker, some states will defer to the next of kin. Other states will require that a guardian be appointed. Often a family member will seek guardianship, but sometimes the court will appoint someone. This person may be a total stranger. So you can see that it

Joanna R. Leefer

is very important to talk with your family members and make sure everyone has a plan in place before the time comes.

FOUR SECRETS ABOUT HEALTH CARE PROXIES/POWER OF ATTORNEY DOCUMENTS

Secret #1: You do not need a lawyer to assign a person to be your proxy. You can do it at any place and time. All you need are two people older than 18 to witness your signature.

Secret #2: Your agent does not need to be a family member. If you are concerned that your son or daughter does not agree with your wishes, don't make him or her your agent. Find a friend, or a professional, you trust to be your agent.

Secret #3: You may cancel the authority given to your agent by telling him or your health care provider orally or in writing. This means that if you no longer feel your agent has your best interest in mind, you can void the agreement.

Secret #4: You can limit or broaden the power of your agent. If you never want to be on feeding tubes no matter what, this is where you can state it. If there are certain treatments you don't want to receive, like dialysis or life support, state it here.

OTHER IMPORTANT FACTS ABOUT HEALTH CARE PROXIES

Before appointing someone as your health care agent, be sure that person understands your wishes. A good way to ensure this understanding is to sit down with your agent and go over your thoughts and illustrate the type of decisions you wish to be made. You might also want to write down your wishes and add them to the proxy, e.g., "I do not want to be resuscitated if my heart should stop" or "if it looks like my coma may be reversible, keep me on life support for at least six months."

Select one person to make the final decision on your care to avoid conflict or confusion among family members and/or significant others. You may also appoint an alternate agent to take over if your first choice cannot make decisions. If you name all your children as agents and each has a different idea of what you want, there can be a great deal of confusion. But if you select one person to have the final decision, it will facilitate matters and cause less contention within your family.

After going to all the trouble of appointing an agent and ensuring that he or she understands your wishes, make sure each of the major parties has a copy of your health care proxy. That means give one to your doctor and other health care providers. Give copies to your agent, your spouse, and your close friends. Also be sure to carry a copy of your proxy in your wallet or purse at all times. To see New York State's go to **www. health.ny.gov/forms/doh-1430.pdf** health care proxy

In other states, look up "health care proxy" or "advanced directives" and the state, e.g., "health care proxy + North Carolina."

T ERMS

Activities of Daily Living (ADLs): A term used to describe activities performed daily, like dressing, eating, bathing, and maneuvering around our environment. Before someone enters a nursing home or receives any kind of care assistance, his ability to do these tasks is assessed.

Alzheimer's Disease (AD): A progressive degeneration of brain tissue that is the most common form of dementia. In the early stages, difficulty remembering recent events is the most common symptom. As the disease progresses, confusion, irritability and aggression, mood swings (e.g., outbursts of fearfulness, anger, or deep apathy), trouble communicating, and long-term memory loss develop. Ordinary daily activities become difficult, accompanied by bewilderment and frustration. Physical problems such as loss of balance, falls, and aspiration pneumonia may occur. Eventually the patient will most likely become totally dependent on care and unable to communicate.

Center for Medicare & Medicaid Services (CMS): A federal agency within the United States Department of Health and Human Services (DHHS). The department administers Medicare programs and works with state governments to administer Medicaid.

Certified Nursing Assistant (CNA): A nursing staff member who works closely with patients and is responsible for basic care services such as bathing, grooming, and feeding. As their name implies, they also assist nurses with procedures, medical equipment, and checking patients' vital signs. Although the length of time in classroom and clinical settings vary from state to state, CNAs must complete a training program and then pass a state evaluation to become certified. CNAs are found in several settings such as hospitals, nursing homes, and home health.

Community Spouse: also called the Stay at home spouse, at home spouse. The spouse that is not ill and is living at home.

Community Spouse Resource Allowance (CSRA): This is the amount of assets the community spouse may retain when the partner is allowed Medicaid. It is approximately 50% of joint income at the time the spouse enters the nursing home, but varies from state to state. The CSRA is usually applied for after the applicant enters a nursing facility.

Comprehensive Care Plan (CCP): This plan is the blueprint for your loved one's care when he enters a nursing home. An Interdisciplinary Team of professionals determines the plan. The team includes nursing, social services, therapy, dietary, activities, and medical representatives. The CCP meeting is typically held within the first 21 days of admission and includes the resident and a family member. The plan must be reevaluated at least every three months to determine if it is still appropriate or if changes should be made. It must also be reassessed if there is a major change in your loved one's condition.

Dementia: This is a general term describing any condition that shows a decline in mental ability severe enough to interfere with daily life. Dementia is not a specific disease but is a set of signs and symptoms. Memory, attention, language, and problem solving are affected. The ability to learn, reason, and remember past experiences is lost. As dementia worsens, individuals typically neglect themselves, become uninhibited and lose control of bowel and bladder function. Behavior may be disorganized, restless, or inappropriate.

Health Care Proxy: A legal document that allows an individual to appoint a trusted individual to make health care decisions for you if he loses the ability to make decisions for himself.

Hospital Discharge Planner: The hospital personnel, often social workers, who are responsible for ensuring that a safe discharge occurs. They can arrange things like home health, skilled nursing facility placement, or equipment needed in the home.

Improving Healthcare for the Common Good (IPRO): A national organization that provides a full spectrum of health care assessment and improvement services that foster more efficient use of resources and enhance health care quality to achieve better patient outcomes. The organization that was founded in 1984 holds contracts with federal, state, and local government agencies, as well as private sector clients, in more than 33 states and the District of Columbia.

Medicaid, Community: A government program that pays for home- and community-based services for individuals who fall below a certain asset and income level. Most Community Medicaid requires the same five-year look back period to qualify for Medicaid assistance. New York is an exception, where income and assets can be transferred in one month and be eligible for Medicaid the next.

This program allows Medicaid beneficiaries to receive services in their own home or community.

Medicaid, Institutional: A government program that pays for long-term services for millions of low-income Americans. The program pays for nursing home care for individuals who are aged, blind, or disabled. Many people become eligible for Institutional Medicaid by transferring most of their assets and income to a third party five years before entering a skilled nursing facility.

Medicare Nursing Home Compare: A government database that gives detailed information on all Medicare and Medicaid-certified nursing homes in the country. The database allows consumers to compare information about nursing homes. It contains a summary of quality of care information on every Medicare and Medicaid-certified nursing home in the country.

Medicare Part A: The federal government health care program primarily for people age 65 and or older. It helps pay for inpatient hospital care, skilled nursing care, hospice care, and institutional services.

Medicare Part B: The federal government health care program primarily for people who are 65 and older. Part B is paid for by the monthly premiums of people enrolled and by general funds from the

Joanna R. Leefer

U.S. Treasury. It helps pay for doctors' fees, outpatient hospital visits, and other medical services and supplies that are not covered by Part A.

Minimum Monthly Maintenance Needs Allowance (MMMNA): A monthly sum of money that Medicaid allows the community spouse (see page 79) or dependents to keep while the ill spouse remains in the nursing home. In order for this provision to take effect, the community spouse or dependents' income must be below a certain limit.

The Nursing Home Survey (NNHS): Every nursing home that accepts Medicare or Medicaid must undergo a state inspection, at least once every 12 to 15 months. A team of three to five state employees who have backgrounds in nursing, social work, dietetics, sanitation, health care administration, and counseling conduct these surveys. Surveyors walk through the facility, observing care delivery, staff/resident interactions, and compliance with standard regulations. Many records such as medical, financial, staffing and equipment maintenance logs are reviewed. A typical survey takes three to five days. The nursing home is cited for any violations and is given a time frame in which the facility can rectify them.

Nursing Home Ombudsman: An individual who works with government agencies to protect the health, safety, welfare, and rights of the elderly in nursing homes. The individual helps investigative complaints, quality of care issues, and financial information. They are advocates for the patient/resident. The representatives must be 18 years or older and must not have a relative or any investment in the facility.

Nursing Home Residents Bill of Rights: A set of federal regulations that ensure the rights and dignity of all nursing home residents. Every nursing home must have written policies that describe the rights of residents. These rights ensure that all residents will be treated with respect and will be kept informed of their treatment plan. The nursing home is required by law to make this policy statement available to any resident who requests it.

Occupational Therapy (OT): The use of treatments to develop, recover, or maintain the daily living and work skills of patients with a physical, mental, or developmental condition. Occupational therapy typically works on upper body functions such as grooming, buttoning or zipping clothes, cooking, and other fine motor skills.

Patient Review Instrument (PRI): A medical evaluation tool that identifies whether an individual is eligible for skilled nursing care placement. The evaluation determines the type and level of care an individual will receive in a nursing home. It will also determine the level of reimbursement rates the nursing home will receive for caring for the individual.

Physical therapy (PT): A series of treatments that help patients develop, recover, or maintain physical functions such as walking, climbing stairs, and balance. The treatment helps restore physical strength and agility that was lost due to accident, disease, or acute illness. Physical therapy typically works on strengthening the lower body or legs.

Pressure Sore: A wound that develops over a bony prominence (e.g., heel, coccyx, hip bone, etc.) related to pressure. When a person lies in one position for more than two to three hours, pressure ulcers can develop. The pressure sore first appears as a red painful area. If pressure is not relieved, the underlying tissue will become damaged and may break open. A pressure sore can become deep (ulcerate) and extend into the muscle and bone. Once a bedsore develops, it is often very slow to heal. Untreated pressure sores can become gangrenous or seriously infected. (Also called a pressure ulcer or bedsore.)

Short-Term Rehabilitation Facility (Rehab): A physical rehabilitation center offering residential services often doubles as a nursing home, though depending on the setup, the patients may be kept separately. These homes are especially good for those who require a substantial amount of physical rehabilitation.

Skilled Nursing Facility (SNF): A residential facility that provides room and board, around-the-clock nursing care, rehabilitation services, personal-care services, medically related social services, and recreational and social activities.

Speech Therapy (ST): Speech therapists work with patients in two areas: language (the ability to speak and understand words spoken to you) and swallowing. Patients may need speech therapy after a stroke or traumatic accident that changes their ability to use language or swallow.

Sub-Acute Rehab: This is slower paced and less intense rehabilitation for patients who cannot tolerate more than three hours of physical therapy daily. This is not usually available in a hospital setting, but occurs in skilled nursing facilities, clinics, and outpatient settings.

BIBLIOGRAPHY

Activities of Daily Living, Evaluation

http://aspe.hhs.gov/daltcp/reports/meacmpes.htm

Bernard Bergman

http://news.google.com/newspapers?nid=1299&dat=19750106&id=AeQ
PAAAAIBAJ&sjid=qosDAAAAIBAJ&pg=6473,94740
http://www .nytimes.com/1984/06/22/obituaries/bernard-bergman-
nursing-home-figure-is-dead.html

Comprehensive Care Plan

http://www.hpm.umn.edu/nhregsplus/NHRegs_by_State/West%20Virgi
nia/west_virginia_comprehensive_care_plans.pdf
http://www .eldercareteam.com/public/577.cfm

Dementia

http://www.mayoclinic.com/health/alzheimers/AZ00028
http://www .alz.org/dementia/types-of-dementia.asp
http://www .alzfdn.org/EducationandCare/musictherapy .html

Joanna R. Leefer

Federal Congress Impoverishment Prevention Provision

http://aspe.hhs.gov/daltcp/reports/spouses.htm

http://www .medicaid.gov/Medicaid-CHIP-Program-Information/By-
Topics/Eligibility/Spousal-Impoverishment-Page.html

http://www .health.ny gov/health_care/

medicaid/reference/mrg/january2 012/page775.pdf

http://medicareadvocacy.org/News/Archives/Medicaid_MedicaidandNurs
ingHomeCosts.htm

Federal Nursing Home Reform Act of 1987

http://www .allhealth.org/briefingmaterials/obra87summary-984.pdf

http://www.aging.senate.gov/events/hr172tl.pdf

Health Care Proxy

http://www .health.ny .gov/forms/doh-1430.pdf

http://www
.medicareinteractive.org/page2.php?topic=counselor&page=sc
ript&slide_id=1335

IPRO

www.ipro.org/

Hospital Discharge Planning

http://www .medicare.gov/pubs/pdf/11376.pdf

http://www .cms.gov/Outreach-and-Education/Medicare-Learning-
Network-MLN/MLNProducts/Downloads/Discharge-Planning-Booklet-
ICN908184.pdf

http://www.caregiver.org/jsp/content_node.jsp?nodeid=2312

Medicare

www.wnylc.com/health/entry/72/

http://www.cms.gov/medicare/provider-enrollment/nursing-homes.html

www.medicare.go

Medicaid, Institutional

http://www .medicaid.gov/Medicaid-CHIP-Program-Information/By-Topics/Long-Term-Services-and-Support/Long-Term-Services-and-Support.html

http://www.health.ny.gov/health_care/medicaid/

Nursing Home Admissions

https://aging.ohio.gov/news/agingconnection/2010April/policy.asp

http://www .canhr.org/factsheets/nh_fs/html/fs_admissionagreement.htm

Nursing Home-Alzheimer's

http://www .alz.org/living_with_alzheimers_choosing_care_providers.asp

http://www.mayoclinic.com/health/alzheimers/AZ00028

Nursing Home Compare

www.Medicare.gov/NursingHomeCompare

Nursing Home Complaints

http://www .medicare.gov/NursingHomeCompare/About/ICInfo/Compl aints.aspx

http://www .health.ny .gov/facilities/nursing/complaints .htm

Joanna R. Leefer

Nursing Home Costs

www .skillednursingfacilities.org/articles/nursing-home-costs.php

Nursing Home Inspection Regulations

www.medicare.gov/nursing/aboutinspections.asp

http://nursinghomes.nyhealth.gov/nursing_homes/about_quality

Nursing Homes—Involuntary Discharge

http://www .theconsumervoice.org/

sites/default/files/advocate/advocacyg

roups/involuntary_transfer_and_discharge_-7-08_update.pdf

http://www .health.ny

.gov/facilities/nursing/rights/transfer_and_discharge .htm

Nursing Home—Ombudsman program

http://www .aoa.gov/aoa_programs/elder_rights/

Ombudsman/index.aspx

http://www.ncdhhs.gov/aging/ombud.htm

Nursing Homes—Readmissions after Hospitalization

http://www .medicare.gov/coverage/skilled-nursing-facility-care.html

http://www.cms.gov/Regulations-and-

Guidance/Guidance/Manuals/downloads/bp102c08.pdf

The Nursing Home Reform Law of 1987

http://www.aging.senate.gov/events/hr172tl.pdf

http://www .allhealth.org/briefingmaterials/obra87summary-984.pdf http://www .aarp.org/home-garden/livable-communities/info-2001/the_1987_nursing_home_reform_act.html

Nursing Home Rehabilitation

http://www .ncbi.nlm.nih.gov/pmc/articles/PMC1403501/

http://www .medicare.gov/Pubs/pdf/10153.pdf

Nursing Home Residents Bill of Rights

http://www.medicare.gov/nursing/residentrights.asp

http://www .ltcombudsman.org/issues/residents-rights

Nursing Home Survey Information

http://www.cdc.gov/nchs/nnhs.htm

http://www .health.ny

.gov/facilities/nursing/about_nursing_home_reports .htm

Patient Review Instruments (PRI)

www .health.ny .gov/forms/doh-694.pdf

http://www .medicaid.gov/Medicaid-CHIP-Program-Information/By-Topics/Delivery-Systems/Institutional-Care/Preadmission-Screening-and-Resident-Review-PASRR.html

Pressure Sores

http://www.mayoclinic.com/health/bedsores/DS00570

http://www .nlm.nih.gov/medlineplus/pressuresores.html

Sub-acute Rehabilitation

http://www .rehabnurse.org/pdf/PRNavigatingRehabSettings.pdf

Joanna R. Leefer

http://aspe.hhs.gov/daltcp/reports/scltrves.htm

http://www .medicareinteractive.org/

page2.php?topic=counselor&page=sc ript&slide_id=8

Made in the USA
Charleston, SC
30 July 2014